What's it like to be ... an ANT?

Jinny Johnson

illustrated by **Desiderio Sanzi**

RiverStream

Hardcover edition published by Amicus
P.O. Box 1329
Mankato, MN 56002

RiverStream Publishing reprinted by
arrangement with Appleseed Editions Ltd.

Printed in the United States of America,
at Corporate Graphics in North Mankato,
Minnesota.

Designed by Guy Callaby
Edited by Mary-Jane Wilkins

Library of Congress Cataloging-in-
Publication Data

Johnson, Jinny, 1949-
  An ant? / Jinny Johnson ; illustrated by
Desiderio Sanzi.
    p. cm. -- (What's it like to be--)
  Includes index.
  Summary: "A worker ant tells the story of her
life, from hatching from an egg to being part of
a colony"--Provided by publisher.
  ISBN 978-1-60753-183-8 (library binding)
  1. Ants--Life cycles--Juvenile literature.
I. Sanzi, Desiderio, ill. II. Title.
  QL568.F7J58 2012
  595.79'6--dc22
                              2011008316

DAD0501
052011

1 2 3 4 5 CG 15 14 13 12

RiverStream Publishing
Corporate Graphics, Mankato, MN
112012—1006CGF12

Contents

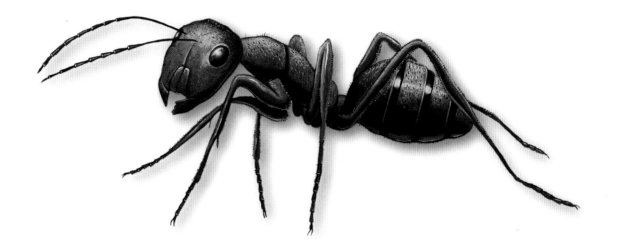

An ant is an insect.

It has six legs and a pair of feelers on its head.

So what's it like to be an ant?

It's hard work being an ant.

I'm busy all the time.

I live in a nest in the woods with lots of other ants.

Our nest is made of dead leaves, pine needles, twigs, and earth.

Inside our nest there are tunnels, rooms, and places to store our food.

Our mother is the queen ant and the head of our family.

She lays all the eggs.

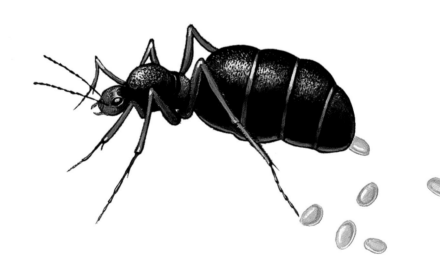

There may be 100,000 ants in a nest.

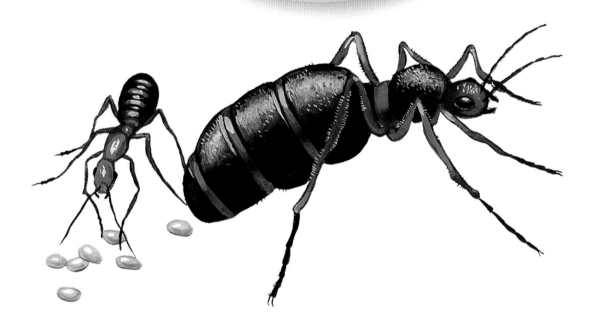

The rest of us look after her and bring her food.

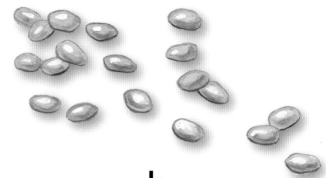

I started life as an egg. It was about the size of a pinhead.

I hatched out into a little squirmy larva.

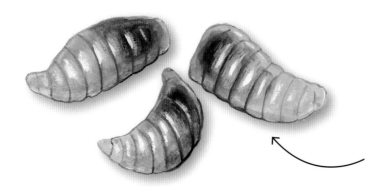

A larva has no legs but can wriggle around.

I grew
until I was about the size
of your little fingernail.
Then I spun a silk case
around myself.

I turned into a young ant inside my silk case.

When I came out, I was a bit weak and wobbly at first.

Other ants looked after me until I could manage by myself.

Then I started work.

I am a worker ant,
like most ants in our family.

*Worker ants
like me don't have
wings.*

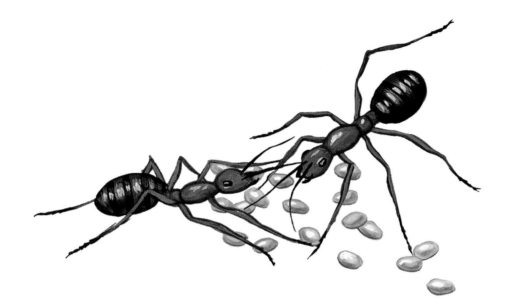

My first job was looking after the eggs and young.

I brought them food and kept them clean.

When I was older I started going out with other workers to find food.

Every day we march off to look for caterpillars and other insects to bring back.

I'm strong. I can carry food that is three times as heavy as me.

We leave a smelly trail so other workers can follow us and we don't get lost.

One day I will be a guard ant and protect our nest.

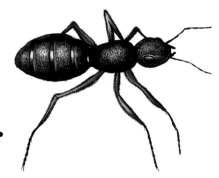

If other insects attack our nest we fight back.

We bite the attackers and spray them with liquid we make in our bodies.

It stings!

The liquid
an ant sprays is called
formic acid.

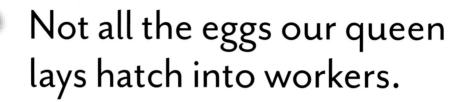

Not all the eggs our queen lays hatch into workers.

Some hatch into male ants with wings.

Male ants don't do any work and are fed by other ants.

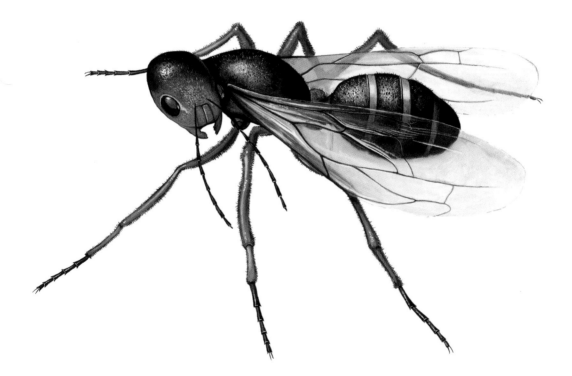

Others hatch into new queens and they have wings too.

One summer day every year
some males and queens
fly out of our nest.

They mate, then the males die.

The queen bites off her wings.
Then she goes back to the nest
to lay eggs or starts a new nest.

More about ants

What are an ant's feelers for?

An ant uses its feelers, called antennae, to smell and taste what is around it. The ant's eyesight is poor but its feelers are very sensitive. The ant can bend them forward or hold them back out of the way.

Do all ants make nests?

Most do, but not all. Army ants are nearly always on the move so they don't make nests. At night they gather round their queen to protect her.

How many kinds of ants are there?

There may be at least 12,000 different kinds of ants and there are probably lots more we don't know about yet.

What do ants eat?

Most ants eat other insects, including other ants! They also eat fruits and vegetables and the bodies of animals that have died.

Ant words

antennae
A pair of long, thin body parts on an insect's head. Antennae are also known as feelers.

formic acid
Stinging liquid sprayed by some ants to warn off enemies.

larva
A wormlike creature. An ant spends the first part of its life as a larva.

queen ant
The leader of the group. The queen lays all the eggs.

worker ant
An ant that gathers food, looks after young and defends the nest.

Ant index

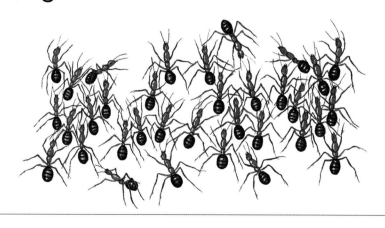